I0802714

!SAFETY CHECK!

STRANGER DANGER

Written by
Valerie
Harvey

KidHaven
PUBLISHING

Published in 2027 by
KidHaven Publishing, an Imprint of Greenhaven Publishing, LLC
2544 Clinton St., Buffalo, NY 14224

Written by: Valerie Harvey
Edited by: Noah Leatherland
Designed by: Jasmine Pointer

Cataloging-in-Publication Data

Names: Harvey, Valerie.
Title: Stranger danger / Valerie Harvey.
Description: Buffalo, NY : KidHaven Publishing, 2027. | Series: Safety check | Includes glossary and index.
Identifiers: ISBN 9781534570665 (ebook) | ISBN 9781534570658 (library bound) | ISBN 9781534570641 (pbk.)
Subjects: LCSH: Children and strangers--Juvenile literature. | Kidnapping--Prevention--Juvenile literature. | Safety education--Juvenile literature
Classification: LCC HQ784.S8 H378 2027 | DDC 649.1--dc23

Printed in the United States

CPSIA compliance information: Batch #CS27KH: For further information contact Greenhaven Publishing LLC at 1-844-317-7404.

Please visit our website, www.greenhavenpublishing.com. For a free color catalog of all our high-quality books, call toll free 1-844-317-7404 or fax 1-844-317-7405.

Find us on

Image Credits:
Cover - Lalavida, New Africa, Touhid Alam. 4-5 - Drazen Zigic, ArtPhoto21, studio marble. 6-7 - annokhotska, ICONO Studio, jujikrivne, outlining. 8-9 - Tatiana Gordievskaia, BearFotos. 10-11 - PeopleImages, Oleg Elkov. 12-13 - ShotPrime Studio, takayuki. 14-15 - FamVeld, Red Cristal, Dwiwahyuf15. 16-17 - Canetti, Krakenimages.com, AhmadRaza09. 18-19 - O.PASH, Vadim Zakharishchev, Uswa KDT. 20-21 - Anna Kondratyeva, Prostock-studio. 22-23 - Wpadington, PeopleImages.

All images courtesy of Shutterstock.com, unless otherwise stated.

CONTENTS

Words that look like <u>this</u> can be found in the glossary on page 24.

WHAT IS A STRANGER?

A stranger is someone you don't know. Most strangers are kind, but some might be unsafe to be around. It's important to know how to stay safe around strangers.

Most strangers are just normal people going about their day.

You can be polite to strangers, but you should always put your safety first. In this book, we'll learn how to recognize strangers, stay safe, and get help if we need it.

It is OK to talk to strangers if a trusted adult is part of the conversation.

NOT ALL STRANGERS ARE SCARY!

Even though we need to be careful, most strangers are not dangerous. Many strangers are regular people doing regular things. You might see them shopping, walking their dogs, or going to work.

Smiling at a stranger or saying hello is OK, but it's important to stay near a trusted adult. Never follow a stranger or go anywhere with them unless a trusted adult says you should.

IF A STRANGER APPROACHES

If a stranger ever comes up to you, pay attention to your feelings. Stay calm, and notice what your body tells you. Does something feel wrong or confusing? You do not have to talk to them.

Move to a safe place right away. Get back to your parent or guardian if you can, sticking to areas with lots of people. If a stranger asks for help, remember that adults should ask other adults, not kids. You are allowed to keep yourself safe.

When you go out, don't wander off on your own.

STRANGERS YOUR AGE

Wanting to make new friends is normal and good. It's safe to play and talk with other children when adults are around. Just make sure you are in safe places, such as schools, parks, or playgrounds.

Never go anywhere with a stranger—even another kid—without asking a trusted adult first.

Even if someone your age seems friendly, always check with a trusted adult before going to play with them. Making friends safely means having fun while staying out of danger.

Stay where a grown-up can see you.

A BAD FEELING

Sometimes strangers—or even people we know—might ask us to do things that don't feel right. They might ask us to keep secrets, go somewhere scary, or do something we shouldn't. If something feels wrong, you don't have to do it.

Always tell a trusted adult, such as a parent, teacher, or guardian, if someone asks you to do something that makes you uncomfortable. Listening to your feelings and speaking up helps keep you safe, even if the person seems nice or tells you not to tell anyone.

Your comfort and safety are important!

SAFETY WORDS

You and your family can create a special safety word. A safety word is a secret password only you and your parents or guardians know. If another adult says your parents sent them to help you, they should be able to tell you this safety word.

Never tell anyone else your secret safety word.

Even if someone knows the safety word, you should still trust your feelings. If anything feels wrong or you're not completely sure, don't go with them. Your safety comes first.

HOW TO SAY NO

You are allowed to say no whenever something feels wrong or unsafe. Start by standing tall and using a strong, clear voice. You can say, "No, I don't like that," or "No, I need to go now." Then, move away and find a trusted grown-up immediately.

You are always allowed to say no.

Remember, saying no can keep you safe. Practicing can help you feel confident and helps you keep yourself safe in real situations.

You can practice saying no in a safe place.

IF YOU GET LOST

If you ever get lost, take a deep breath. Look for safe strangers who are there to help. People in uniforms, such as store workers, firefighters, or police officers, can be good options. Your parents or guardians might have ideas about what kind of strangers to look for when you need help, such as parents with children.

Go to someone who is helping others. Tell them your name and that you're lost. Then, stay where you are. Remember, trust your feelings. If someone doesn't feel safe, find a different helper.

If you know a trusted adult's phone number, try calling them.

THE SAFETY CIRCLE

You can play a safety game with your family! First, draw a big circle on the floor. This is your Safety Circle—your special safe space. Then, talk about different situations together.

Ask yourself how safe you would feel in each situation. If you feel safe, stand inside your circle. If you don't, step outside.

Playing this game helps you learn what feels safe before something happens. You've got this!

Knowing who to trust helps you stay safe.

A SAFETY STAR!

You've learned so many smart and brave ways to keep yourself safe—from using your Safety Circle to trusting your feelings and finding safe helpers. Being a Safety Star means remembering these tips and practicing them whenever you need to.

You can be a Safety Star!

You can also shine by sharing what you know with your friends. When everyone learns how to stay safe, you help make the world a kinder, safer place for everyone.

GLOSSARY

conversation when people talk and listen to each other

guardian an adult who takes care of someone and keeps them safe

password a secret word or code

regular something normal or usual, not special or different

uniforms clothes people wear to show what group they are part of or what job they have

INDEX